fast
thinking.
crisis

PEARSON EDUCATION LIMITED

Head Office:
Edinburgh Gate
Harlow CM20 2JE
Tel: +44 (0)1279 623623
Fax: +44 (0)1279 431059

London Office:
128 Long Acre
London WC2E 9AN
Tel: +44 (0)20 7447 2000
Fax: +44 (0)20 7240 5771
Website: www.business-minds.com

First published in Great Britain in 2001

© Pearson Education Limited 2001

The right of Ros Jay to be identified as Author
of this Work has been asserted by her in accordance
with the Copyright, Designs and Patents Act 1988.

ISBN 0 273 65305 9

British Library Cataloguing in Publication Data
A CIP catalogue record for this book can be obtained from the British Library

10 9 8 7 6 5 4 3 2 1

Typeset by Pantek Arts Ltd, Maidstone, Kent.
Printed and bound in Great Britain by Ashford Colour Press, Hampshire

The Publishers' policy is to use paper manufactured from sustainable forests.

fast thinking: crisis

▶ deliver bad news

▶ manage tough situations

▶ limit the damage

by Ros Jay

contents

introduction

Don't panic! There you were, carrying on as normal when out of the blue … disaster. Computer crash? Half the department off sick and it's the day of the big launch? Food poisoning in the canteen? Redundancies? Customer collapsed in reception? There are so many possible crises that it's amazing really that they don't happen more often. But thank goodness they don't.

And were you ready for this one? No, of course you weren't. It wouldn't be a crisis if you were prepared, would it? It would be routine, and you wouldn't have needed this book. As it is, you just want to get it over with as quickly as possible and get back to normal. Well, you've come to the right place. This book will get you through any crisis fast, because once you've learnt the basic rules for crisis handling, you can apply them to every disaster.

That's lucky because, when a crisis hits, your top priority is not generally to send out to the bookshop. So the bulk of this book will help you with those crises that, like it or not, take a little longer to resolve. For example:

- the after-effects of natural disasters – fire, flood and storm
- redundancies
- sackings (the crisis being their impact on the remaining team members)
- computer or switchboard crashes
- chronic staff shortages
- product recalls
- strikes and other industrial action
- pollution (when it's your fault)
- morale crises (such as the team's failure to win a crucial contract)

... and all the other crises, which you can't think of now, but that will certainly happen to someone sooner or later, and it could be you.

This book will also help you prepare for future crises of the more immediate kind – the ones where you don't have time to read a book first:

- fire
- serious injury
- sudden illness
- missing vital equipment on the morning of the launch or exhibition
- bomb scare.

If you use this book as a preparation, you'll find that when disaster strikes you're far better equipped to cope. And the sections at the back on crisis handling in an hour and crisis handling in ten minutes flat will get you through even the most urgent crisis at the speed of life.

Of course, the aim is not simply to come out the other side alive. You may have thought that would do, and indeed it will do far better than *not* coming out alive. But we can do better than that. With cool, well-thought-out crisis handling (no, that's not a contradiction in terms), you can come through disaster looking even better than you did before you started. Don't believe me? Read on …

Whether you have a day to prepare or only a few minutes, you are going to have to think fast. Not only fast, but smart too if you're going to hit the ground running. You want:

▶ **tips for looking as if you know more than you do**

▶ **shortcuts for doing as little preparation as possible**

▶ **checklists to run through at the last minute**

… all put together clearly and simply. And short enough to read fast, of course.

So whatever the crisis, don't panic. I know that's like saying that if you scratch a mosquito bite it'll only itch more. Easily said, but not so easy to do. But really, you've nothing to panic about, because everything you need is in this book. And nothing else. You have here a fast but comprehensive guide to becoming an expert crisis handler within the next hour.

▶ work at the speed of life

This book will take you through the key stages of crisis handling:

1 You'll have to begin by defining your problem (not as obvious as it might seem) and setting priorities accordingly.

2 The next step, for all but the most immediate life and death crises, is to hold an emergency planning session. You might do this on your own but you are far more likely to involve others too.

3 After this, it's time to crack on with the disaster recovery operation. You can't do it all yourself so you need to allocate tasks and, crucially, you have to allocate the right tasks to the right people.

4 Throughout the operation, it is essential to adopt the right attitude towards everyone involved. People skills are key to creating a success out of a crisis. So we'll look at the guidelines for keeping everyone positive and motivated.

5 Some crises have a PR dimension, as news of them spills over into the outside world. The press will want to know all about the toxic waste you've been leaking into the local river system or the redundancies you're making. Getting the press on your side is an important part of your role as crisis leader.

6 And finally ... when all the tasks have been completed and life is back to normal, you need to acknowledge that the crisis happened and tie up any loose ends.

This book will take you through the key stages of crisis handling

fast thinking gambles

When a crisis hits, you've no choice but to scramble your resources and handle it as best you can. With the help of this book, you'll come through it with the least possible fuss and the greatest possible credit. But you are still, inevitably, merely turning off the fan and scraping off the walls whatever it was that hit it.

How much better to turn off the fan before impact. When you think on your feet, you can never come up with as many options as when you think with your feet up. So in the long term, it's wise to put your feet up and think through how you will handle future crises. Make a crisis plan. You'll find out how to do this as you go through the book but, in case you need any convincing, here are a few reasons why it's better not to leave everything until you hit red alert:

- Many crises can be planned for, and it saves you a huge hassle in the event if you already have a back-up system in place.

- Whatever the crisis, you can work out a set of priorities that you simply and speedily apply in every case – for example, what are the most essential items in the building to rescue in any kind of physical catastrophe, from storm damage to bomb scare?

- Even when you couldn't have predicted the disaster, you can still shortcut the recovery process if you have planned which personnel you will allocate to which type of task (maybe Jake is great with people or Phil is your best problem-solver).

- Planning may not give you every answer, but it can highlight problems that you might otherwise miss in the heat of the moment. For example, if your plan draws attention to the fact that your most essential electronic machinery is in the basement, you're less likely to forget, as the burst pipe drenches you on the second floor, that your priority is to get downstairs fast and protect the hi-tech equipment in the bowels of the building.

Fast thinking will pull you through any crisis with panache, but if you want to lead your team through it rather than be pulled through, you need to back up your fast thinking with forward planning. That way, you'll be so cool in a crisis you'll make 007 look like an amateur.

When you think on your feet, you can never come up with as many options as when you think with your feet up

1 define your problem

So you've got a problem? That's putting it mildly. You've got a crisis. A major-panic-stations-drop-everything-oh-God-what-are-we-going-to-do disaster. And the first thing you're going to do is stop and think.

If you have someone collapsed on the floor in front of you, unable to breathe, you should act immediately. For any other kind of crisis – however disastrous – you should take at least a few moments to think before you do anything else. This has two particular purposes:

- ▶ It means that when you take action it is far more likely to be the right action, rather than simply action for the sake of it.

- ▶ It helps you to stay calm. Instead of rushing headlong into panic, a moment of reflection will stabilize your emotions.

PLAYING BOWLS

Taking a few moments to think when a crisis hits keeps everyone else calm too. They will be so impressed by your cool approach – like Sir Francis Drake playing bowls as the Spanish Armada approached – that they will be filled with confidence in you and your ability to handle the situation.

So what are you supposed to do in these few seconds or minutes of reflection? Just stare at the walls trying to conceal your mounting panic? No, there is a more useful train of thought than that. You need to define the problem. It may take seconds or it may take minutes (if you have them). But it must be done.

You might think that when a major water pipe bursts, when the computer crashes or the truck delivering everything for the exhibition breaks down a hundred miles back along the motorway, it would be blatantly obvious what the problem is – the building is filling up with water, we have no computer or there's no exhibition stand.

However, these are not the *real* problems. They are the problems too many people focus on exclusively in a crisis, but they are actually disasters

only because of their knock-on effects. Let's take the computer crash as an example. This is a crisis because it means:

- **you can't take orders**
- **you can't fulfil orders**
- **you can't issue invoices**
- **you can't generate a despatch list**

… and so on. These are your real problems. If your computer crashed but you had a simple mechanism for duplicating all the computer's functions in some other way, it wouldn't be a crisis, would it? It would be just a glitch.

So your priority when the computer crashes is not to get it fixed, but to get the orders out on time. Obviously getting the computer fixed is a great way of achieving this, but it is only a means to an end, it is not the end in itself. Your top priority should be to find a temporary way of getting orders despatched, and worry about fixing the computer later.

If you don't take time to identify your real problem, you are likely to put all your energies into fixing the computer instead of getting the orders sent out. That's why you need to spend a few

minutes identifying the real problem first so you can invest your resources wisely in resolving it. Here are some more examples:

- ▶ **When the building floods, the real problem is that valuable equipment or stock is being damaged and that work is being disrupted.**
- ▶ **When the exhibition stand doesn't turn up, the problem is that you can't sell your organisation and its products or services so effectively to the visitors.**
- ▶ **When you have a chronic staff shortage, the problem is that your team can't perform certain specific basic functions or can't perform them as effectively as it should.**

PRIORITIZE

So that's your first step: define your real problem so you can focus your resources on it. The next step follows on naturally: set your priorities. As you can see from the previous examples, a single crisis can generate a raft of problems. A burst water tank in the roof causing a flood might generate several problems:

- ▶ **valuable equipment is being damaged**
- ▶ **expensive stock is being ruined**
- ▶ **work is being disrupted.**

One of the defining laws of crises is that there are never enough resources to go around. So where are you going to concentrate your efforts? Saving your equipment? Rescuing your stock? Keeping work flowing – and if so which work most needs to carry on regardless? You must decide which of your problems is the most pressing, so you can put your scant resources to the best use.

thinking smart

URGENCY OVER IMPORTANCE

Keep in mind that the most pressing tasks in a crisis don't have to be the most important ones – they are the most urgent ones. For example, if your computer is likely to be back in action within a day or two, processing orders might be able to wait quite easily and catch up later (so long as you can take the orders manually). On the other hand being unable to generate pay cheques until two days late could have far greater repercussions.

And that's the point of defining and prioritizing your problem. Instead of fixing your crashed computer in half a day and losing half a day's work, how much better to spend a whole day sorting it out but to achieve it without losing any work at all.

II

LONG STOP

The planning process may lead to setting up a permanent fallback position. You can install automatic back-up computer or website systems in case of failure. You could build up a list of emergency staff to call on when you have a staff shortage. Or you might consider it worth having a spare exhibition stand and displays.

for next time

FOR NEXT TIME

You're never going to have a lot of spare time when a crisis hits – not this time, next time or the time after. So you need to find time *before* there's a crisis. This logic is not as flawed as it seems, for one simple reason: few crises are as unpredictable as we make out.

All right, there are some crises for which we simply can't prepare. I know someone who was trapped in a lift for two hours with about a dozen other people. Among these were a small child, who was sick after the first few minutes, and a woman who was phobic about vomit. Obviously you can't be expected to plan for this sort of emergency. I also know of a business where a horse was found inexplicably wandering in a third-floor corridor. And one where an irate

customer decided to embarrass the staff by stripping stark naked in the middle of a busy shop.

But you can plan for a lot of other emergencies. Hold a session with your team to plan out your priorities in any likely crisis. In each case define the problem and identify your priorities. When the crisis occurs, you'll have your answers ready. OK, not every crisis will happen, but sooner or later at least one of the ones you've prepared for is likely to – and you'll be ready for it. We already prepare ourselves for what we will do in the event of fire: here are some ideas of what else to plan for:

- ▶ Computer crash – if your business relies on a computer, sooner or later it will let you down, you know it will.
- ▶ Physical damage to the buildings – this is relatively common too. It might be a major storm, a burst water pipe, or a fire in a neighbouring building which doesn't require immediate evacuation, but could eventually spread.
- ▶ Bomb threat – some organisations, such as public transport companies, utilities, theatres, galleries and cinemas, are particularly vulnerable to this. If you are a likely target you should be prepared.
- ▶ Dangerous chemicals – if you keep these on site, you should plan what happens if there is a spillage, a fire or if you pollute the local watercourse.
- ▶ If you keep valuable materials or equipment in a vulnerable place – a basement with a risk of flood or a building that is exposed in the event of extreme weather conditions – think through what you need to focus on in an emergency.

- ▶ If you use dangerous equipment on site that could cause serious injury, be prepared.
- ▶ If you manufacture potentially dangerous machinery or equipment, be prepared for product recalls.
- ▶ If you're planning an exhibition stand and there's any potential for a major catastrophe, such as the stand supplier letting you down or a vehicle breaking down with disastrous consequences, be ready for it.
- ▶ If you have a busy period for staffing coming up, such as a special event or a peak ordering time, plan what you will do if a severe flu bug strikes and 50 per cent of your staff are off sick.
- ▶ If you run a website that is important or even central to your business, don't be caught on the hop when it crashes or your server goes down.

Many organisations also have their own specific potential disasters, which you need to identify. In each case define your problem and set your priorities in advance, when you can think clearly, so you save yourself time when it really happens.

The process of thinking through these potential emergencies will show up all sorts of things you can do now to minimise the damage when calamity knocks at your door.

2 emergency planning

Now you know exactly what problem it is you're tackling, and what your priorities are. But you still have to decide *how* to deal with the problem. Again, if you have a serious accident on your hands, call an ambulance before you do anything else. But for most crises, however urgent, you will need to hold an emergency meeting. Even a serious accident calls for an emergency meeting if it is an ongoing crisis (for example, if people are still trapped). Just hold the meeting *after* you've called the emergency services.

Hang on. A meeting? Are you kidding? One of those interminable things we managers spend all our time in, where people talk for hours and nothing gets done? Surely meetings are a waste of time even when you *have* time to waste. Isn't it the very last thing you need in a crisis?

Well, that sort of meeting would be, yes. But that's not the sort of meeting you're going to hold. You're going to hold a quick – if necessary, very quick – meeting that is directed entirely towards generating fast action. No, that's not a contradiction in terms; this sort of meeting is perfectly possible.

ASSEMBLE YOUR TEAM

When you find yourself in the midst of a crisis, you have to scramble everyone who is available until the crisis is resolved. But although the entire organization might be involved in some way, they cannot all be part of the crisis team. Trying to recover from a disaster whilst co-ordinating a team of five hundred is a cumbersome and slow process. And you ain't got that kind of time. So you need a select crisis team around you who can, if necessary, mobilize other forces when they need to.

Generally, your crisis team will consist of your immediate team. Or, if you manage several teams, it might be the team most immediately involved in the problem. Whoever your team is, you want about half a dozen people at the centre of this recovery operation. So call them all together for an emergency meeting.

thinking smart

II

SHOW THEM THEY'RE IMPORTANT

In an ideal world, you'd have about four or five people around you. But you may not be inhabiting an ideal world – if it were an ideal world it wouldn't have a crisis in it, after all. If your immediate team has, say, seven or eight people in it, you may have to involve them all. If you leave out a couple of people they will feel deeply unwanted, and it is generally better to involve them to keep them motivated and feeling valuable.

SUMMARIZE THE SITUATION

It might seem redundant to summarize what is happening but, in fact, it's easy to assume everyone knows the score when they don't. Even if they realise the computer has crashed or half their colleagues haven't turned up for work, they still need to hear it from you. And they need you to tell them the implications. They may have forgotten that today is supposed to be the day for the pay cheque run, for example.

Only by stating clearly the problem and its implications can you be absolutely certain that everyone is as clear as you about why this is a crisis. And when you're co-ordinating a crisis

24

operation, it is even more essential than ever that everyone is working to exactly the same set of information, rules and priorities. Even a slight wrong move now could turn a crisis into a disaster.

This is especially true of those crises where staff morale is involved. Suppose you are about to make several staff redundant, or perhaps your bosses are. You'll need to get together with colleagues for a crisis meeting (with a little less urgency than if the building were on fire, but no less importance). If you aren't all giving exactly the same version of events to your teams, rumour and gossip will quickly spread and you'll have a nightmare to deal with. So it is always worth summarizing the situation.

This summary may take only a few seconds: 'OK guys. The computer's down and we don't know yet how long it will take to fix or how much data we've lost, if any. So we can't process orders or issue invoices, and we've no idea what orders we're supposed to be despatching today.'

DEFINE THE PROBLEM AND SET PRIORITIES

You have probably been through this process already, as we saw in the last chapter. If so, tell your team exactly what the real problem is, and the priorities as you see them. But check to see if anyone else has identified any further problems or

priorities that you hadn't got covered. Maybe you've been dealing with a couple of major complaints this morning and now can't access the customer data to resolve them – that could be a priority you'd overlooked.

BRAINSTORM YOUR OPTIONS

Get everyone to come up with all the ideas they can for coping with the problem (the *real* problem, that is). If you have identified several problems, spend as long as you've got – even if it's only a minute or two – on each of the priorities in turn (starting of course with the top one).

thinking fast

AN AIR OF AUTHORITY

You'll have to adopt a brisk, confident tone for this meeting, but not a domineering one. You have two considerations to balance: on the one hand, you want to transmit an air of urgency (without panic), so people don't think they can spend hours debating the finer points of the problem. This is a meeting on the hoof, not a sit-down discussion. On the other hand, you don't want to squash valuable contributions before they are even uttered by implying there's no time for anyone but you to speak.

Maybe you could take orders manually over the phone. Or explain the problem to customers and arrange to call back when the computer is fixed, and take the order then. You could still take urgent orders manually. Or you could invite phone customers to fax an order through.

When it comes to despatching today's deliveries, maybe you could identify them by going through the paper copies of the invoices sent when the order was made. Perhaps you have a lot of regular customers and can call them up, explain the problem and ask if they have a delivery due in the next few days. Or perhaps your best option is to give up trying to meet deliveries, wait for customers to call in a couple of days to ask where the delivery is, and then courier the packages to them.

The brainstorm session needn't take long, but may bring to light all sorts of ingenious ways round the problem, or at least ways round part of it.

DON'T TAKE UNNECESSARY DECISIONS

You haven't got time to waste, so don't do anything that doesn't *have* to be done. This includes not wasting time taking decisions you don't need to. So don't say: 'We'll just take customers' phone numbers for now, and see if we can get the

computer back by lunchtime. If we can't, we'll start taking orders manually this afternoon.'

Why decide now what to do this afternoon? By lunchtime you might have established that the computer will be fixed by half past two. Or you might already have arranged two hundred call-backs to take orders. Or only four. You don't know until lunchtime what you will do then if the computer isn't fixed, so don't worry about it now. For the moment, simply decide to take phone numbers and to review things at lunchtime.

ALLOCATE TASKS

By now, your meeting should have been going on for no more than ten minutes. If you're really pushed, it may have taken as little as two minutes to get to

NO 'WHAT IFS'

As a rule of thumb, never take a decision that is dependent on information you don't have. No 'what if' decisions. The only proviso here is that you shouldn't take a decision now that will back you into a corner if certain events ensue. So don't agree to promise customers you'll call them back tomorrow if it's possible you still won't be able to take their orders then.

here. Now it's time to start sorting out the crisis on the ground, so you need to allocate tasks to each of your team. You may allocate tasks directly, or you may allocate responsibility for tasks that the team members can delegate – or both, of course. The next chapter is all about allocating tasks as effectively as possible, so we won't waste time on it here.

CHECK EVERYONE UNDERSTANDS

The impulse now is to tell everyone to get cracking. But there's one last thing before you close the meeting. Make sure everyone is entirely clear about the problem, the decisions you've just taken, and their own tasks. If you don't, catastrophe may follow as people misdirect their energies, waste precious minutes on the wrong activities, or duplicate each other. In the worst instances, they may even make things worse.

Suppose you ask your team to evacuate everyone from the building into the car park because someone's phoned to say there's a bomb in the cafeteria. In the rush, one of your team evacuates all the customers into the staff car park – which is next to the cafeteria – instead of into the public car park. They heard the words 'cafeteria' and 'car park' and, in their panic, put two and two together to make three and a half.

So it's vital to recap and check people understand clearly, especially if they may be panicking and therefore not thinking as rationally and clearly as usual. Showing people that there is always time to check that everyone understands helps to calm them down, and reassures them that it's OK to ask if they are in doubt.

◀◀ for next time

Print out an emergency meeting aide-mémoire and keep it to hand for the next time you have to hold a crisis meeting. It should read:

- ▶ Summarize the situation and its implications.
- ▶ Define the problem.
- ▶ Set priorities.
- ▶ Brainstorm the options.
- ▶ Make any necessary decisions – and no others.
- ▶ Allocate tasks.
- ▶ Check everyone understands.

Hold a crisis planning meeting every year with your team to talk through what you should do in each of the crises you have already decided to plan for (the ones we identified at the end of the last chapter). In effect, hold the crisis meeting for each of these potential emergencies. This will save you loads of time when they happen, as well as pointing up any yawning flaws in your system. 'You mean if the computer crashed we'd have no way of knowing which orders to send out? We should do something about that before it happens.'

You need to repeat this exercise every year or everyone will forget there even *was* a plan by the time the next major crisis hits. And if they do remember, they'll find that the key contact person left the organisation two years ago or the plans for evacuating the building involve mustering everyone in the car park that disappeared last year when you built on the new engineering workshop (which doesn't feature in the evacuation plans either). So update your crisis plans annually.

Make sure everyone is entirely clear about the problem, the decisions you've just taken, and their own tasks

3 allocating tasks

Coping with a crisis is all about action. As we've seen, the more thinking time you can muster the more streamlined and effective your actions will be. But most of the exercise is likely to consist of doing rather than talking. Even with a morale crisis you have to decide on a plan of action, which is likely to involve calling people together for briefings or establishing new ways of working. In a short-term emergency you'll be doing anything from mopping out the basement to cobbling together an exhibition stand from empty cereal packets and sticky-back plastic.

So if it's action you need, you'd better make sure it is the right action, and carried out by the right people. Your emergency crisis meeting should have identified the key tasks by defining the problem and setting priorities. You know that you need to evacuate the top floor, persuade the directors to staff the sales office because no one else is

available, move all your sensitive equipment away from the danger area or get a replacement demo model sent over from Hull.

For speed, you will also have to allocate groups of tasks to responsible people who can cope with them. For example, you might allocate to one or two people the job of clearing out the basement or getting the pay cheques produced manually. These jobs will incorporate several tasks, which you haven't time either to identify or to allocate individually, so they need to be taken on by people who can use their initiative in identifying the individual tasks themselves and getting them done.

thinking smart

HANDING OVER THE REINS

Sometimes you're not the best person to be in charge of the crisis operation. I know you're the boss, but maybe your marketing manager is better equipped to handle the situation. Or your shop manager, or your computer expert. So delegate: your most important job is to decide who to put in charge. Then get out of the way. Don't abdicate responsibility; be around if they need you. But let *them* make the decisions.

Don't get bogged down

Someone needs to keep an eye on the overall picture and co-ordinate the whole crisis operation. And that someone is you. You need to be available so that:

- ▶ **You know what is going on.**

- ▶ **People can come to you with fresh problems (just what you need) or ideas (that's more like it).**

- ▶ **You have time and a clear head to keep on top of the operation, make decisions and call any review meetings you consider necessary.**

This means that you should do your best to avoid taking on any other important tasks yourself. If fixing the lorry is the only thing that will save the situation and you're the only trained mechanic available, I guess you'll have to do it. But otherwise, stay free of any tasks that require concentration.

This doesn't mean you have to do nothing at all. Your most sensible course is to be an available pair of hands for a task that doesn't have to occupy your brain and that you can stop at a moment's notice if something that needs your attention crops up. So help out with mopping the floor, moving equipment, digging out paperwork – something menial. Your staff will love you for it, too.

DON'T TREAD ON TOES

If you're doing something manual, which you can abandon when you need to, you'll presumably be working on a task allocated to someone else. Maybe you've put Liz in charge of moving all the equipment and you're shifting all the archive disks. In this situation, remember who is in charge. Liz. Don't try to take over – otherwise when you're called away Liz will be left at a distinct disadvantage, not to mention being mightily hacked off with you just when you need her support and enthusiasm. You're just an extra pair of hands for Liz. You're only the manager in charge when something outside the equipment rescue operation crops up.

WHO GETS WHICH TASK?

So to whom are you going to give each task, or group of tasks? Well, I obviously can't answer that precisely because I don't know what your crisis is or who you've got there to choose from. But there are certain types of people and there are certain types of task. And you should aim to pair the right person with the right task.

So here's an outline of eight key types of people you do (or don't) want around you in a crisis, and which type of task to give them. Identify as many of them as you can within your team.

1 **The 'yes' person.** It's worth having someone who takes directions well next to you in emergencies. If you say: 'Call an ambulance' or 'Move those things onto the top shelves first', they do it. Some people will respond with: 'don't you think a doctor would do?' or 'Why don't we move these ones before those ones?'

There are times when people can help by coming up with better ideas than your own, but in an emergency the speed of the decision is often more important than its precise nature. If you think on your feet pretty well it's going to be a fine line between which decision is best, and action is better than debate. A reliable yes person at your side will not only get on with carrying out your instructions, but in doing so they will set a good example to the rest of the team.

2 **The cool-headed person.** This is the person to put right in the thick of things. They may be good at thinking on their feet, or they may not. It doesn't matter. You can tell them what to do if they're not a great decision maker, you just need them to do the nerve-wracking jobs. They are probably your first aider. If not (you may be lucky enough to have more than one cool-headed person on your team) they can assist the first

aider, or be the one to check there are no customers left in the building when you evacuate.

3 **The decision maker.** Often in an emergency there are two places where things are happening; the fire is on the first floor and the people evacuating the building are being checked and counted in the car park. Or someone has to go and stop the flooding while someone else starts to limit the damage. You can't be in two places at once so you need someone to go and be you somewhere else.

4 **The panicker.** This is someone to get out of the way as fast as possible. Problem is, you can't tell them that. So find a plausible job that needs doing urgently and that gets them out of the way: 'Pat, Robin's not going to be able to fix this leak without some tools. Can you go and see what you can find?'

5 **The gregarious one.** Some crises can be solved only by asking for outside help. Someone needs to call the stores and plead for spare hands to help move the equipment away from the flooding, and beg an emergency plumber to come round within half an hour – failing that they need to see if anyone in any other part of

DECIDING ON A DECISION MAKER

Your decision maker should not only be adept at thinking on their feet, they should also carry authority in the team. This could be because they are older or more senior but it doesn't have to be – they may simply be someone the team has a natural respect for. That way there are no arguments when you say: 'Would you three please go and help Robin evacuate the second floor.'

the organization happens to have plumbing experience. Some people are particularly good at this – they know who to call and they don't mind asking favours.

6 **The genius for detail.** If someone *knows* that their job is to stand next to you and tell you what you've forgotten to do, they're much more likely to think of things you've missed. For this role you need someone who is going to limit themselves to important things, but it's invaluable having a team member who occasionally reminds you that if there's a power failure, that means the electronic gates in the car

park won't open for the fire engine, or points out 45 minutes into stemming the flood that it might be wise to cancel this afternoon's appointment with your top client *before* they leave their office to come and see you.

7 **The problem solver.** How are you going to get that machine clear of the flood when it's too big to go through the door and up the stairs? Leave it with the problem solver – and an assistant if you can spare one – while you get on with sorting everything else out. This kind of problem can take up too much of your time in an emergency, so give it to someone else.

8 **The sympathizer.** It's often vitally important to have someone to calm people down – to reassure customers who are being evacuated because of fire or to hold someone's hand while they're waiting for the ambulance. This is not a job to give to whoever hasn't got anything else to do. It's a skilled role and some people are far better cut out for it than others. It may even be something that your panicker is good at once their initial shock has worn off.

BUILD A STRONG TEAM

When it comes to dealing with the crisis there are no hard and fast rules because it depends so much on what exactly the emergency is. But things will go far more smoothly if you follow these guidelines for which roles to allocate to which team members. In general, a strong team that is used to working together will always cope better in a crisis – even a totally unrehearsed and unanticipated one – than a weak or disparate team or group.

This is because each member understands their own role and function and their relationships with each other, so they can short-cut past many of the

thinking smart

LET EVERYONE HELP

Some crises are over in an instant and take only one or two clear-headed people to deal with them. But some last longer – perhaps you need to ask for volunteers to stay late or work over the weekend cleaning up your flooded basement and rescuing your sensitive electronic equipment. In these cases it's important to involve everyone, or the ones you leave out will feel they're not wanted. So find ways to make everyone feel they helped save the day.

◀◀ for next time

Plan in advance the best people to fill each type of role in an emergency. When you hold your annual crisis planning meeting (which I mentioned at the end of the last chapter), this is a useful exercise to go through with your team. If everyone has agreed who the 'decision maker' is, for example, they will feel involved and loyal when this person's skills are put into play in a crisis.

It should go without saying that not all the roles we have covered in this chapter should be discussed openly among the team. Identify your 'panicker' in advance, but keep it to yourself. The key roles to agree with your team are:

- cool-headed person
- decision maker
- gregarious person
- problem solver
- sympathizer.

When it comes to it, the more aware people are of their primary role (everyone's secondary role is to do anything else that's needed) the more smoothly they will work together, the more valuable they'll feel and the more effectively they'll solve the problem.

There is another vital step you can take to prepare in advance for a crisis: make sure your own team has at least one qualified first aider. Don't simply ask for volunteers, though. Draw up a list of people in the team who are usually on the premises, and then cross off the names of all those you suspect would be likely to go to pieces in an emergency.

communication barriers that confuse or slow down other groups of people. For example, a good team will instinctively turn to the most appropriate person to take control, regardless of seniority, where a disparate group will often fail to 'appoint' a suitable leader.

thinking smart

DON'T PUSH IT

You can't force people into something like being a first aider; they need to be enthusiastic about it. So if someone prefers not to do it, move on to the next person on your list and ask them.

will always cope better in a crisis

You now have a viable list of potential first aiders. Decide who would be the best in a crisis and ask them if they would be happy to train.

If groups within the team are often elsewhere – for example they attend a lot of trade shows with heavy display stands to set up – you may decide that one of them should also take first aid training. After the course, it can be very helpful to ask the new first aider to talk to the team about the main things they got out of the course.

Take their training seriously. I can tell you from personal experience that if your organisation sends you on a one-day first aid course and never mentions the fact again, five years on, if faced with someone who has stopped breathing or is bleeding profusely, you haven't got a clue what you're supposed to do. First aid training has to be topped up regularly.

4 setting the right tone

You would have thought that having to cope with the crisis and sort out the practical problems surrounding it would be enough for you. But oh no. You don't get off that easily. Managing a crisis is one of those situations that makes you feel that either there isn't a god or, failing that, we're saddled with a god who has a wicked sense of humour.

You see, the way you handle this crisis not only affects the outcome of the crisis itself, it will also have a huge impact on the morale of your team and on your position within it. Whether you lead a team of five or five hundred, these few hours will set a pattern that will be very hard to change in a hurry. Handled badly, this crisis will lose you respect, loyalty and the morale of your team. But handled well (which is how you're going to do it), it will boost your team's enthusiasm, reinforce its identity and confirm you at the head of it.

So this chapter is all about the psychology, if you like, of handling a crisis. How to get your team behind you and keep it there all the way. This is especially important in the face of crises that damage the team's morale, such as sackings, a death in the team, collective failure and so on. So the second part of this chapter focuses on these kinds of emergency situations.

THE BLITZ MENTALITY

A crisis generates heightened emotions, from excitement to fear. And you know yourself that you are far more sensitive when you are in an emotional state. So your behaviour now will make a strong impression on everyone. The right approach will pull the team together and make it stronger for the future as well as for now.

A blitz mentality often develops in which the group has no choice but to pull together, and its identity is positively reinforced. Often, people's positions in the team are strengthened as their colleagues discover talents in them they never knew existed. Someone senses a new admiration as everyone discovers that they speak fluent Polish, that they can memorize half a dozen phone numbers on the spot or that when the keys to the company car go missing in an emergency, they know how to hotwire the ignition.

NOT A LOT OF PEOPLE KNOW THAT

A crisis is a great opportunity to bring out hidden talents in your team. The traditional team roles largely break down under pressure and become much more flexible. So if someone volunteers for a job you wouldn't normally have associated them with, try to give them a chance. It could work wonders for their morale.

But the wrong attitude can create strong resentments, splits in the team and a blow to morale. And the key to the whole thing lies not in what action you take, but in how you communicate. So you need to follow the seven key rules of communicating with your team in a crisis, to make sure you keep everyone pulling together.

THE SEVEN RULES OF CRISIS COMMUNICATION

So here they are: the seven core principles for making sure the team you're leading through the crisis comes out stronger at the end of it.

1 **Keep everyone informed.** Make sure you pass on any relevant information to your team throughout the crisis. Don't wait until your next

crisis meeting tomorrow morning to tell them something they need to know now. Ignorance and misinformation lead to mistakes during a crisis.

For example, if you know that the roof of the engineering block is unstable due to last night's major storm, don't rely on everyone following your general instruction not to go in there. Tell them it's unstable. Otherwise someone might decide to use their initiative and go in to check the electrics are turned off or to rescue expensive equipment or vital data files.

2 **Assemble the team together to give important information or instructions.** We all know how to play Chinese whispers, passing a message along the line until it becomes distorted beyond recognition, but this isn't the time for it. The only way to be certain that everyone has the same information, and is working to the same set of instructions, is to collect them all in one place and talk to them all at once. Do this even if the switchboard is down and this means that the one incoming line you've rigged up can't be answered for five minutes while you brief the team. In the long run, you will save time, as well as further problems.

WORKING BRIEFING

If you really can't afford to stop work for a second, you can talk to people while they work – but *only* if the work is so mindless they can listen easily while they're doing it: get them all moving piles of books or bailing out with buckets while you talk to them.

3 **Encourage your team members to ask questions.** I know you want to get the briefings over with as fast as you can and then get back to work. But if people aren't allowed to ask questions – at the briefing or one-to-one – they may get their facts confused, fail to understand the priorities, or misinterpret your instructions. Don't forget, some of your team may be panicking, and that does nothing to aid clear thinking. If you don't allow them to ask questions, time consuming though it may seem, you are asking them to tackle the crisis armed with incorrect information, false priorities and faulty instructions. Is that really wise?

4 **Involve people in key decisions.** This is the ideal approach, because if people are involved they feel committed to the decision and

GENTLE TONES

When you talk to your team, try to be aware of your tone of voice. You may be out of breath, worried or up against the clock, but it is your job to stop your team from panicking. So don't let them hear anything in your voice that might alarm them. Let them see that *you're* not panicking, so why should they?

responsible for making it work. Obviously, you cannot, in the thick of things, start organizing questionnaires and focus-group meetings to discuss the best solutions to your crisis. But make sure you go as far as you can to involve people.

If you are responsible for tens or hundreds of people, you generally can't involve them all. But usually you can involve your immediate crisis team in most decisions. 'Who thinks we should call an ambulance, then?' may not be a wise decision to try to share, but you can ask for input on whether you should put your energies into replacing the exhibition stand or whether to forget the stand and worry about replacing the display materials instead.

When you have more time – in those equally critical but slower moving crises – you can certainly involve people in decisions. For example, if a member of your department has died, you can consult their colleagues about who should attend the funeral.

5 **Be available.** If the crisis you're dealing with is in any way upsetting or emotionally charged – anything from a damaged building to asking people to work unscheduled overtime – your staff may need to talk to you. They may be worried, frustrated, upset, even angry. If they feel they can't approach you because you're too busy for them, they will be alienated and demoralized. So make time for them to get their feelings off their chests, or to ask your advice, or just to have a whinge: they need you.

6 **Show your staff that you're on their side.** Make sure everyone who works for you knows that their welfare is a top priority. Let them see that you are working to rescue their property, to get a decision on overtime out of top management or to get their project deadline extended. If they can see that you're working for them, they'll be keen to work for you in return.

7 **Never lose your sense of humour.** Laughter is the best way in the world to reduce stress. If you join in or even initiate the humour, the rest of the team will see you as being even more cool and in control. And it takes the pressure off them because it indicates that you're not about to bawl them out for the slightest mistake.

Unless this is a life or death crisis, it's worth keeping in the forefront of your mind that in the long term, the team is more important than the crisis. Yes of course you need to get the website up and running again or the building restored to

thinking smart

UNDER THE MICROSCOPE

If you're smart, you'll have noticed that the key rules of communicating under pressure are key rules for communicating all the rest of the time as well. They just matter more in a crisis because everything is magnified – emotions, results (good or bad) and everyone's level of attention. This is why good managers are generally good in a crisis too: they may not necessarily be the world's most cool-headed people, but they instinctively foster a positive attitude in those around them.

normal or the exhibition stand erected. But by next week or next month, the crisis will be all but forgotten. The team, however, will still have to work together. So generating a positive and enthusiastic atmosphere, which binds everyone together, is critical to the future of the team.

A CRISIS IN THE CAMP

This is especially true when the crisis is one that affects the team as a unit. Many of the crises that fall into this category are ones that last for days or even weeks, rather than hours. But they are still serious crises and are worth discussing on their own here because their impact on the long-term welfare of the team can be huge. The kind of crises I'm talking about are, for example:

- ▶ redundancies;
- ▶ major overstretching of the team – excessive demand for overtime, for example;
- ▶ major change – from a corporate merger or restructure to an office move or relocation;
- ▶ bad news – the team can't have the resources it wants to complete a project successfully or the department's request for more office space has been turned down;

- ▶ **team failure – to win a contract or meet a vital project deadline, or maybe the team's negligence has caused a serious accident;**
- ▶ **theft in the department;**
- ▶ **death or serious illness in the team;**
- ▶ **disruptive office affairs (which can reach crisis point);**
- ▶ **sacking a member of the team.**

All of these have long-term repercussions even if the initial crisis is relatively short-lived. So you need to make sure that you deal with them in a way that strengthens the team or department, rather than undermines it. The seven rules of crisis communication, which we've already looked at, are critical here, but there are other guidelines you'll need to bear in mind too, depending on the kind of problem. So let's look at each type of crisis in turn.

Redundancies

You presumably can't prevent the redundancies, so the way to keep this crisis to a minimum is to handle it sensitively and to recognize that even those people who are not made redundant feel threatened – next time it could be them.

- ▶ Keep everyone fully informed from the earliest stage possible. Don't wait until you have more information. People always get wind of trouble and their imaginations will blow it up into something bigger than it really is, so you're not protecting them by keeping quiet.

- ▶ Don't just tell them the basics – tell them whatever they want to know. How many redundancies? What departments? What are the criteria for deciding who should go?

- ▶ Don't, however, give them guesses. If you haven't got the information, you can try to find out, but don't speculate. They'll take it as gospel, having nothing else to go on.

- ▶ Once the redundancies have happened, assemble the rest of your team. Reassure them that you are now a smarter, tighter outfit than before. And give them any genuine reassurances you can that they are not about to go the same way.

Overstretching the team

Your team or department may be overstretched because of unreasonable demands from senior management or because of long-term absence by someone in the team – because of illness, for a sabbatical or on maternity leave, for example.

- ▶ Be available. Yes, this is always important but especially so here. It's not just that people are working harder, they are often doing jobs they are unfamiliar with or at speeds they are unused to. So they may well need more

understanding, may need to ask a lot of questions or want help with prioritizing.

- Be prepared to lower your standards. Again, if people are trying to do more work in the same length of time, something may well have to give. Accept that not everything can always reach the same standard it does when the team is relatively relaxed.

- Share the extra workload. If someone is away, say on maternity leave, and you are sharing their tasks between the rest of the team, take some of them on yourself. Or you could free someone else up to do extra by relieving them of one of their regular tasks – though not their favourite one or one that means a lot to them for status reasons or whatever. To be safe, ask them: 'I could probably take over some of your work for a while so you're free to look after Angela's customers as well as your own. Is there anything you'd like to pass on to me?'

- Do something about the workload where possible – and be seen to be trying to reduce it. Sometimes the pressure lasts for a predetermined length of time. But sometimes it can go on indefinitely. Eventually your words of

thinking smart

STATE OF EMERGENCY

When your team is working under any kind of long-term stress, recognition is vital. Acknowledge that they are under pressure and give them plenty of thanks and rewards.

sympathy and understanding will begin to sound hollow and the team will start to feel that, as long as you keep telling them they're wonderful, you think that excuses you from ever having to do anything about the problem.

Managing change

This could be caused by mergers and takeovers, restructuring, new legislation that affects the team's working practices, relocation and so on.

- To start with, warn the team of impending changes as far in advance as possible, and fill them in on all the details you can.

- Involve them in any decisions you can by holding team meetings and inviting comments, questions and suggestions.

- Encourage people to express any negative feelings and listen sympathetically – they may resist change because it threatens their security, because they know they are slow learners or because they think it will make their role less important or their job less stimulating. Ask them to be very specific about their objections.

- Deal with each objection individually. Naturally there will be some genuine disadvantages resulting from the changes; admit to these but explain how they are more than offset by the benefits.

- When the changes are made, make regular checks with the resistors to see how they are adapting. Keep doing this until they tell you they are settled.

A PROBLEM OR AN OPPORTUNITY?

Some people love change and revel in the challenge of it. You have to make sure that these team members don't either belittle or leave behind the people who are more resistant to change and who regard it as a crisis to be endured rather than a challenge to be surmounted.

It's worth examining the office move briefly, because it's something that most team leaders find incredibly frustrating. An effective group of people will handle the practical side of the move with little difficulty; the disruptive nature of the process is caused by status issues rather than operational ones. These can reach crisis dimensions, causing splits and ructions within your department, if you don't handle them sensitively.

- Some desks or offices are considered more 'important' than others. But the argument never admits this – it's always conducted in operational terms: 'I need to be near the car park to carry in boxes of samples' or 'How can I conduct selection interviews in an open-plan office?'

- It's rarely any use bringing the status subtext out into the open; people always deny it. But if you are aware of it you can often adjust some other status factor upwards: the

person's name on the door, their own business card, a change of job title from 'operator' to 'executive' or something else that will placate them.

- Take into account that status doesn't float in mid-air: it is relative to the people around. So it may be that the only reason John isn't happy with the office you allocated him is because he doesn't think it's as good as the one you allocated Pat, and he sees his role as being just as important as Pat's. In this case, you can use the same approach, but if you also give Pat business cards or a new job title you won't have achieved anything. Try to give these kinds of rivals completely different status symbols so it becomes hard for them to compare themselves with the other person. Which is better, a plusher office or a better sounding job title? Hard to say really – and hopefully John and Pat will find it pretty hard to say too.

Bad news

- You won't be moving to the smart new offices after all – your team is one of those staying in the grotty old building.

- You've been through the budget and there's just no way you can find the money to take on a temp for three months to help get a key project finished on time; the rest of the department is going to have to carry all the extra workload itself.

- The board has just announced that it is planning redundancies, which will probably affect your team.

Some types of bad news affect everyone and it's not a pleasant task having to break it to them. Their morale is likely to be seriously damaged and it can take a while to rebuild it. So you need to be as positive as possible when you tell them the bad news – within reason: unbounded cheerfulness and optimism would be out of place.

- ▶ Tell them the reasons why the decision has been made. If you didn't make it yourself, find out the reasons from whoever did.

- ▶ Let them know that you are sorry they missed out, and that you feel they deserved to move into better offices or to have extra help on the project. However, the wider picture didn't allow this to happen.

thinking smart

THE VALUE OF DISTRACTION

Following bad news, try to give your department another challenge to put their energies into, preferably something you are pretty confident will work out well. For example, if your team has a real talent for organizing and giving presentations, try to arrange a key presentation sooner rather than later after bad news, to help distract them.

- Sometimes compensation is an option. For example, if they can't move offices perhaps you can arrange to refurbish the present ones. Or if you can't afford a temp for three months perhaps you *can* afford to contract out at least some of the work.

Failure

Sometimes bad news isn't simply a matter of bad luck. Perhaps the team has lost a contract they've been working to win for months, for the simple reason that their pitch wasn't as good as their competitors'. Or your team's negligence caused four deaths when a car crashed through a safety barrier that should have stopped it – your team built the crash barrier and never noticed the fault. All the points above apply, along with a few more techniques.

- Don't try to cover up failure; admit it. 'We failed.' Make it clear that *you* are not displeased with *them* – after all, you're one of them. Let them see that you recognize that as team leader you carry the greatest responsibility.

- Your job, in relation to your own superiors, is to take the blame yourself but to give credit to your team and its members (as the old army maxim says: there are no bad soldiers, only bad officers). Your team members need to know that you are in it with them, and that you aren't putting the blame on them when you talk to people outside the team.

- Hold a session to analyze the mistakes or weaknesses. Point out to them that if you can learn from your mistakes you should be better than anyone next time – you'll be the last people to make that mistake again. But it's crucial to identify and accept your failings.

- Once the team has done this, remind them that nothing is all bad. There must have been some things that you did well and you need to know what they were so you don't reject them along with the mistakes. This gives you a strong positive note on which to end the crisis meeting.

- Once a day or so has gone by, start to joke about it. You might as well – you've got nothing to lose. It keeps the atmosphere light and shows your team that it may not be good to fail, but it's not the end of the world. It will ease the pressure on everyone. There are a couple of points to bear in mind:

  - be wary of joking about a failure that has led to serious illness, injury or death;

  - don't direct jokes against any member of the team (except yourself, if you wish);

  - don't make jokes that reinforce the team's sense of inadequacy. Every joke has a butt, so try to focus your joke on things like the competitor that won the contract, the specification for it, any minor mistake that was caused by the whole team and not just one member, minor details that were out of the team's control – anything else but the team and its members.

Theft

Theft is a matter for the police; it's not your job to find the culprit, although clearly it *is* your job to do anything you can to help the police find them. The potential crisis in the team arises when there is a suspicion that it is an inside job – one of your team may be the thief.

- You must carry on as normal. Pass on to the police – in confidence – any information you feel may be useful, and leave it at that. Keep your eyes open, but don't go rummaging in people's desks when they're not there or manically checking up on their petty cash records. They'll realize instantly what you're doing.

- If your team members think for a moment that you don't trust them, it will do virtually irreparable damage to your relationship with them. Then, when the culprit is caught, all the innocent members of your team (which may well be every one of them) will have to work with you knowing that you considered them all capable of theft from their own employer. If you only suspect one or two of them, who turn out not to be guilty, your relationship with them will be even worse.

- Set your team an example. Until proven otherwise, your attitude must be: 'None of my team would do this. We'll be vigilant, but since none of us is guilty we shan't allow it to get in the way of our work.'

Death or serious illness in the team

This is about the most shocking thing that can happen in a team, and one that needs to be handled very delicately. Your team members will be at their most sensitive and will judge you harshly for any insensitivity you show. Having said that, don't be too nervous – they will see that you're stunned too and they will forgive you any mistakes made through being shell-shocked or inexperienced in dealing with this.

- When you hear the news of death, accident or diagnosis of serious illness, call the whole team together and tell them all at once.

- Be prepared for some colleagues to be extremely upset; if you have a company counsellor or doctor, arrange to have them on hand. If the news is unexpected and shocking, give the person's close colleagues the rest of the day off – maybe longer. Never mind what happens about today's important meeting or presentation: if the team think you put work before people they will lose respect and loyalty towards you in a big way. And the strength of the team is more important than whatever is in the diary for today. Just about anybody will understand your cancelling an event or appointment, or shutting up shop for the day, because of serious accident or death.

If your team members think that you don't trust them, it will do virtually irreparable damage to your relationship with them

BE GENEROUS

If you're not sure what concessions to make to the rest of the team, or what action to take towards the injured person or the family of an employee who has died, always err on the side of generosity. Whether you're considering how much time off, how big a wreath to send or whether to send gifts, no one's going to complain about a generous decision, but they won't like feeling that they work for a skinflint.

▸ **If the person has died, give their fellow team members time off to go to the funeral, and go to it yourself. Make sure the organization sends flowers, quite apart from anything that members of the team may do jointly or separately.**

▸ **Give the team plenty of time – maybe several weeks – to get back to normal (depending on the nature of the tragedy). Let them feel they can talk about it – don't allow it to become a taboo subject.**

▸ **If you make any mistakes, say so: 'I'm sorry I didn't give you all the day off on Friday. With hindsight I can see that we were all much more shaken than I realized at the time.'**

▸ **If one of your team members is diagnosed seriously ill, but is still working, let them decide how to play it. They may want to keep it quiet or they may wish to tell people themselves, singly or as a team. Or they may want you to tell the team.**

Affairs

One of your team is having a fling with one of the directors of the company. Two married team members are having an affair. What do you do about it?

▶ The good news is that 95 per cent of the time you do absolutely nothing. It's not a crisis at all. In fact, it's none of your business.

▶ It only becomes a crisis if it seriously interferes with the department and its work. Maybe there's a suspicion that one of the team is being given special treatment because they are involved with someone higher up the organization. Perhaps they are even viewed as a management 'spy'. Worse still, if one or both of the people involved is married, someone in the department may have spilt the beans to one of the partners. That can really cause team relations to hit crisis point.

You'll have to take the person – or people – on one side and let them know that you're not happy about the effect this is having. If two team members are involved talk to them separately, not together, since each one is independently contributing to the problem. They might also feel inhibited and unable to talk freely in front of each other.

▶ Behave as though the affairs weren't happening, in terms of how you treat the people concerned. If the rest of the team think that one of their colleagues suddenly has more clout with you just because they have a special relationship

with a member of senior management, you will lose the loyalty of the rest of your team. Let everyone see that it makes no difference and there shouldn't be a problem.

(▶) The other occasional, and certainly uncomfortable, situation you may encounter is when two of your team have a relationship with each other and then split up acrimoniously. Worse still, the rest of the team may even take sides. Again, talk to the two people separately and let them know that they are damaging the team and they must resolve things, at least while they are at work. Tell them you hold them at least partly responsible if their colleagues take sides.

Then speak to the other members of the team one at a time, briefly. Tell them: 'It's none of our business what is going on privately between Robin and Kim, but I am making it clear to everyone on the team, including them, that it mustn't get in the way of work. If you have an opinion on the subject, I'd like you to forget about it during working hours. I understand that this may not always seem easy, but it's important for the good of the team.'

Sacking a team member

(▶) In the unlikely event that you have to dismiss a member of staff, talk collectively to the rest of the department after the person has left. Tell them that you regret that it had to happen and there was nothing personal in your decision. Explain that you dismissed the person because their presence in the department was preventing the team from achieving its full potential – their colleagues were probably well aware of this and will understand. If it's appropriate, point out that the person was not a failure in themselves, they were merely unsuitable for the team.

▶ Let them know that you are confident that you were acting in the best interests of the department as a whole and you are sure that now they will be even more successful. You feel that all the remaining members are valuable to the team and each has an important contribution to make.

It's not always pleasant or easy to deal with these difficult situations, but remember that it's often just as bad for the rest of the team – and sometimes even worse for them. So always treat them with respect, even when you're under immense

thinking smart

KEEP MUM

Whatever happens, don't give members of your department any confidential information about their ex-colleague's misbehaviour. Quite apart from any legal implications, they will assume that if they ever leave the department you'll feel free to give away their confidences too.

pressure, acknowledge their difficulties and give them credit afterwards for handling the situation so well. When things ease off and you have the chance to breathe again, you will find that if you've handled the problem effectively your team will be even closer and stronger than it was before.

for next time

FOR NEXT TIME

Learn the seven key skills of crisis communication and practise them in your everyday approach to work. That way, when the next crisis strikes, you'll find it far easier to keep your team right behind you.

fast thinking pause

Have a break, we're nearly there.

Acknowledge your staff's difficulties and give them some credit afterwards for handling the situation so well

5 handling the press

Everyone loves a drama – except perhaps the people caught up in it. Inevitably, then, many crises will attract the attention of the press. They gather like hyenas around the kill, each hungry to get first bite at the story. And not only do you have to deal with the crisis itself, you also have to cope with the press, ready at any moment to turn on you if you make a wrong move.

The press can be either a blessing or a curse in a crisis, and the balance can lie in how you handle them. Of course, sometimes the press are on your side from the start. If your buildings have been damaged by severe weather or a lorry has careered off the road straight through your shop window, you have the sympathy of the media from the outset.

But the press always want someone to blame, and all too often they will pick on you. If you're making redundancies, if you've polluted the river that runs past the factory, if an accident has been caused by faulty equipment – they'll be sniffing round for evidence to pin the blame on you.

GETTING IT RIGHT

So what can you do? The good news is that there is a wealth of advice, derived from the experience of thousands of organizations over many years. There *are* ways to handle the press (and other media), which will at least minimize the damage and at best turn their attitude around to one of support for your case. So here are the key rules for handling the press in a crisis.

Keep in touch

Tell the press what's going on right from the start. Keep them sweet by holding press conferences; don't wait to be asked. Get outside the front gates and tell them what is happening. The more information you give them, the less they will need to dig the dirt to get a decent story. Don't wait until you've resolved the crisis – keep them posted from the moment they turn up asking questions.

The press can be either a blessing or a curse in a crisis – it's up to you

REMEMBER YOUR OWN

It's no good keeping the press informed if you don't also keep your own people posted. Otherwise disgruntled staff, who are being kept in the dark, may well decide to pass on to the press their own outdated or misunderstood version of the facts.

Be honest

Remember Richard Nixon? If you get caught lying, you're done for. It's *never* worth the risk.

UP FRONT

Many years ago, the BBC accidentally double-booked two key political figures to give one of the prestigious Reith lectures. One had to be cancelled, of course, and the press were full of how and why he had been snubbed. The Director General of the BBC adopted a simple, but ingenious, approach when questioned by the press. He just said: 'It was a cock-up, OK?' He was open, honest and wrong-footed the press completely. We all have cock-ups from time to time and the press understand that as well as anyone.

Keep it simple

There are three rules to remember to keep things simple. (I know there should only really be one. Sorry.) First: the press don't know your organization or your industry as well as you do and they want to print a clear, simple story for their readers. So don't confuse them with unnecessary details, jargon or background information they don't want. Just keep your message uncluttered. If they ask for more, give it to them if you can. But don't volunteer it.

The second rule of keeping your story simple is to make sure you have only one spokesperson if you possibly can. Otherwise there is a danger that they may contradict each other. One single point of communication means one single, consistent voice.

And the third rule is: never speculate. This simply adds to the confusion. Speculation may be reported as fact – it often is. So if you're asked to guess at the cause of the chemical leak, how many redundancies there are likely to be or when the building will be operational again, politely decline to comment. Or just say, 'I don't know.'

So these are the three rules of keeping it simple:

One single point of communication means one single, consistent voice

1 Don't give more information than you need to.
2 Have a single, consistent message delivered by a single spokesperson.
3 Never speculate.

Get your priorities right

You will horrify readers, listeners or viewers if you start to talk about the financial cost of this disaster when people have been killed or injured. Likewise, they aren't concerned about your faulty equipment when you've just killed all the wildlife for a ten-mile stretch of the river. So talk about the crisis in the light of the public's priorities. These are:

1 people
2 environment
3 property
4 financial implications.

Be aware how things look to other people

Be aware of what the public perception of your crisis handling will be. It's not enough to be right – you have to be *seen* to be right. Suppose a press story breaks reporting that many supermarket eggs are infected with salmonella and there is a slight risk of serious illness. You are an egg producer. If you react by insisting that there is no danger at all,

people will just think: 'They would say that, wouldn't they?'

There may indeed be no danger – or there may be. It doesn't matter. What matters is that people will *think* you are trying to cover up the facts for your own ends; that you're prepared to lie to people about their health rather than lose profits.

So consider how your version of events, which people will consider potentially very biased, will look. Better to say that you are very concerned about the health scare over eggs. You have no evidence that there is any risk at all, but you're taking action to find out the facts as fast as possible. Support any research – maybe donate funds to it – and invite inspectors to check out your operation. Say you would welcome official guidelines on how your organization can remove any risk and generally be seen to be taking the action the public wants, not just paying lip service to it.

Be positive

If you seem worried or downbeat in interviews, people will assume you're in trouble. If you come across as angry they will take a dislike to you. People will read a great deal into your attitude, so make sure it is always friendly and positive, especially when you're talking to the broadcast

NEVER 'NO COMMENT'

What do you think when you hear an interviewee say 'no comment', or when a report says that 'the company declined to comment'? You think they're guilty, don't you? You reckon they've got something to hide. That's what everyone thinks. And it's what they'll think about you, if you say 'no comment'. So don't. If there's nothing you can tell them, it's better to say: 'I'm afraid I don't have any more information at the moment.'

media. If people have suffered, it doesn't do to look too cheerful about it, of course. But you can still be open and courteous. Make sure you show sympathy for any victims of the disaster, whether or not you accept responsibility.

Be friendly

The press are only doing their job. If you want them on your side, you need to accept this and not hold grudges against them. Let them use the phone and the cafeteria (if it can cope), and give them a warm room if the weather's atrocious outside and you can spare one.

Always treat the press politely and with respect, whether or not they show you the same courtesy. Be as helpful as you can in giving them press packs, background information or whatever else they ask for.

Get your friends on your side

If the press are against you, recruit people outside the company who will speak on your behalf. Satisfied customers, trade association contacts, suppliers, ex-employees … anyone to whom the press will be interested to talk and on whom you can rely to back you up. They will assure the press that your safety standards are exemplary, that you're a great company to work for, that you are known for your reliability or whatever it is you need said. Outsiders always have more credibility than insiders.

thinking smart

GAGGING ORDER

There are some people you just know are going to put their foot right in it. Maybe they have a grudge against the organization, maybe they love gossip or maybe they just don't know when to shut up. In a crisis – or preferably before it – identify these people and keep them away from the press. Do whatever you have to. Send them on an impromptu business trip to Sydney or Rio de Janeiro if you must, but don't let them speak to the media.

Go the extra mile

If you've made a mistake, or are believed to have made a mistake, do everything you can to put it right. Even if people blame you for the crisis itself, don't give anyone an excuse to complain about your response to it. Do even more than you have to. Give people extra time off, replace their damaged property without quibble, even upgrade it, pay to clean up the river *and* fund a new wildlife reserve along its banks. Show that you're sorry you messed up, but you genuinely want to make everything better.

Remember, you don't have to deal with very many crises (thank heaven), but the press deal with them for a living. They are bound to be smarter than you at it, so don't try to fool them – they'll make *you* look the fool. Just play it straight, honest and open.

NEVER A BAD WORD

You may remember a few years ago a cross-channel ferry ran aground on a sandbank. Due to the vagaries of the tide it was a day or so before they could float it off again. Meantime everyone was stuck on board. But the ferry company and the crew leapt into action as soon as the disaster struck. They kept everyone informed, refunded the cost of the tickets, gave away all the free food and drink they could and generally bent over backwards to make up for the discomfort and inconvenience.

When the ferry finally docked, the press were waiting to interview the passengers as they disembarked. But much to their disappointment (I should imagine), they couldn't find a single passenger who had a bad word to say about the ferry operator. They all insisted, 'It was just bad luck, and they looked after us beautifully.'

If you've made a mistake, do everything you can to put it right

Either you or your organization – or both – should be prepared for dealing with the press. You may not know what kind of crisis will strike, but you know sod's law states that it's only a matter of time before something hits the fan.

The more high-profile your organization, and the greater the potential for disaster, the further you should go to prepare for it. But however small the risk of a PR disaster, you can still take some steps to prepare. The process is a valuable exercise in itself, focusing your mind on possible dangers and on how you might handle them.

Here are the key steps well-prepared companies or departments take to limit the damage in the event of a crisis:

- You will need a spokesperson to talk to the press, so decide ahead of time who it will be. Maybe you'll have more than one person standing by, according to the nature of the disaster. Train this person (or people) in how to deal with the media.
- We've already looked at preparing a list of 'likely' crises. Once you know what these are, you can also write the press releases in advance. Just fill in the gaps when the time comes, so you won't have to cope with writing a press release from scratch as the flood waters are rising.
- You can also prepare any other letters that the press might want to see, such as product recall letters to customers and so on.

- ▶ Prepare emergency press packs with details of your safety record, your evacuation procedures and so on. Make sure these are checked, and updated if necessary, every year.
- ▶ Think about how you would manage a horde of media people invading your premises. Where would you set up a press room? Could the cafeteria cope?

You can take all these steps fairly quickly and they will be invaluable when you need them. Go through the planning process with your team and it will help them to be prepared in an emergency, too. Just make sure everyone understands that the key thing is to treat the press warmly – however hard – and try to win them over to your side.

Just make sure that everyone understands that the key thing is to treat the press warmly – however hard

6 handling the aftermath

It's all over. The pollution wasn't nearly as bad as everyone first thought, the flood waters have receded, the website's back online, the redundancies are completed or the exhibition went amazingly well and your makeshift stand was a hit with your sympathetic customers.

So that's it. Or is it? Well, not quite. Before you settle back to work as if nothing had happened, there are still some loose ends to tie up. When the crisis is over, it's time to consider the people involved in it.

You're not the only one who has spent the last hour, week or day in a state of crisis. All around you, your colleagues, and maybe members of the public too, have been suffering as a result of the emergency you've just come through. Or perhaps they've been rallying to your side and helping you to get through the crisis quicker and more smoothly. Either way, you need to acknowledge them.

SYMPATHY MESSAGES

If people have suffered, they will be hurt if they feel you've forgotten them as soon as the crisis has passed. So make a gesture of sympathy now and it will count for a lot. Maybe it's a case of sending a card or a note, or perhaps a bouquet or a bottle of wine. It depends on the circumstances – err on the side of generosity. If someone has to spend six months in bed following an accident on your premises (even if you weren't to blame), a get well soon card might seem a little lame. Perhaps financial help might be better or a new, large-screen television to keep them entertained while they're laid up.

If customers have been put out by delayed deliveries or unrepaired faults, again you should get in touch. Offer them a discount on their next order, send them a bottle of champagne or invite

thinking smart

GET PERSONAL

If you have business customers, do something for the customer personally rather than for their employer. A discount does them no good at all – it's not *their* money you're saving. Send them a personal gift instead.

them to your next shindig, at the same time as sending them a note thanking them for their understanding. They'll probably end up more loyal than before.

SAYING THANK YOU

The people who helped you get through the crisis want and deserve your appreciation. It's probably the only reason they worked their socks off in the first place. So don't be coy about it. Tell them how wonderful they are. And to show you're not just being glib, tell them exactly how they were so wonderful: 'I don't know how you kept all those customers calm' or 'Where did you learn so much about electrics? We'd have been lost without that.'

Don't just tell your team how great they were. Tell everyone else too. Send a special report praising them to the board of directors, write an article for the corporate newsletter, put them forward for a corporate award.

And give them a thank you present. If they worked together to get the computer back up, take them all out for a slap-up meal. If they saved half a dozen lives, buy them a car. Match the reward to the action. But make sure you reward them.

Post-crisis recovery

If your switchboard crashes and takes the best part of the day to fix, you can assume that life will be back to normal by the following day, barring any backlog of calls that still needs clearing. But some crises take time to recover from and you need to be ready for this.

Not surprisingly, the hardest disasters to get over are those that leave people injured or dead and the ones that involve deep human emotions such as loss, failure, guilt and the like. You cannot expect your team to get over the failure of a major project or the responsibility of having caused major pollution in only a day or two.

So what should you do? Give up? Of course not. Pretend the crisis never happened? No, it would demoralize the team still further if you appeared to deny their feelings. Here are a few guidelines, then, to get you through the recovery period:

- ▶ Once the immediate crisis is over, call everyone together and explain that you recognize that things are tough at the moment, but it's time to get back to work as usual. Be sympathetic but upbeat. Tell them that the team is strong enough to come through this.

▶ Be understanding and sympathetic towards your team and let them feel they can talk to you. Don't give the impression that the subject is closed. The crisis may be over, but their concerns are an ongoing issue.

▶ Be prepared to lower your standards a little. If it takes a while for your staff to recover their previous level of efficiency, don't be too tough. Just make sure the trend is upwards.

thinking smart

DON'T LET GO OF THE REINS

Don't be tempted to slacken off too much, soften the rules or change the system (except to prevent a recurrence of the crisis). People need the consistency of a structure and a system they recognize to give them confidence and security at a difficult time.

So there you have it: crisis handling. With the help of this book you should sail through this crisis and every other one, closely followed by a strong, effective and loyal team. And when it's all over, I hope your boss buys you a bottle of wine, at the very least.

There's one last thing you need to do. Sit down with your team, once the dust has settled, and analyse what went wrong and how you handled it. You're not trying to allocate blame and the mood of the meeting should be upbeat and positive, without fear of recriminations, otherwise you'll have wasted all the good feeling you generated when you thanked everyone.

But you do need to establish two things:

▶ Can we reduce the risk of this crisis – or a similar one – happening again?
▶ Another time, could we handle it any better?

If you don't learn the lessons of this crisis – about what you are good at, as well as where your weak spots are – you won't find the next crisis any easier to handle. So reap the benefits of hindsight and use them to prepare the ground for the next crop of emergencies.

If you don't learn the lessons of this crisis you won't find the next crisis any easier to handle

crisis in an hour

Don't panic. This is luxury. A whole hour to prepare for a crisis? It can happen. Many crises take a while to get off the ground: suppose you've just had half your department call in sick on the day of your big product launch. You've probably got an hour or so before your customers and the press turn up in which to avert the catastrophe. Or maybe your boss has just called to tell you that there's going to be an announcement at lunchtime about the restructuring – and your department's in for a big shake-up.

So what do you do when you have a brief warning of an imminent crisis? You might have forty minutes, or you might have two hours. Either way, how can you best use the time to turn the crisis into no more than a bit of a drama?

1 You'll need to begin by defining exactly what the problem is, as we saw in Chapter 1. For example, it's not that you are short-staffed, it is that you can't give as impressive and slick a launch presentation as you wanted, you can't show each visitor to their seats personally, you can't provide refreshments during the mid-morning break.

2 Call together your immediate team – assuming the crisis isn't confidential at this stage. Hold an emergency crisis meeting (see pages 22 to 31). If you aren't able to talk to your team at this stage (or if they're *all* off sick) you'll have to work through this process on your own.

3 Begin by identifying the top priorities – is a slick presentation more important than the refreshments, for example?

4 Now brainstorm ideas for resolving the problem. Suppose someone nips out now and buys cold drinks and juices for everyone – then no one would need to make teas and coffees mid-morning. You could just set out an unstaffed refreshment table. As for the presentation –

think through which sections or visuals might need to be cut if there's no one to operate the equipment. Or is there time to train someone else up quickly?

5 Delegate everything you possibly can, following the guidelines on allocating tasks (see pages 32 to 43). You need to be free to co-ordinate and deal with any other problems that come to light over the next hour, so don't get bogged down in jobs you don't have to.

6 Make sure you are somewhere everyone can find you fast if they need to. Don't disappear.

7 Remember the seven rules of crisis communication (see pages 46 to 52) and follow them to the letter, and you should come through this as smoothly as anyone could.

Remember the seven rules of crisis communication

crisis in ten minutes

You are moments away from disaster. In ten minutes the flood waters will be lapping round your ankles, half your shop-floor workers will walk out or five hundred guests will turn up to a dinner that won't be cooked because power to the kitchens has just failed.

Terrific. It's not as if you didn't have enough to do already ... and now this. You'll definitely hand in your notice next week. But you'll still have to deal with this first. So what can you do? You've got ten minutes, and you can't afford to waste even one of them. So here's the form:

1 Take a long, slow, deep breath. Literally. Calm the initial rush of adrenalin before you start to act. Five seconds of inaction will set you up to stay cool and set a calm example to everyone else.

2 Identify the real problem underlying the crisis (see pages 14 to 17).

3 Remember the key priorities for dealing with any crisis: people first, then the environment (if that's an issue here), then property, then money. So the first thing to ask yourself is whether there are any people at risk. If so, forget everything else while you deal with that and get them to safety.

4 Once there is no risk to people, identify your priorities. If there is more than one problem, decide which you will address most urgently.

5 Think. Alone or with your team, think through your options. There is an overpowering urge in an emergency to do something, no matter what. But it *does* matter what. It is a tough, but necessary, part of crisis management to quell this urge and take a few moments to think calmly.

6 Take firm control and delegate as many tasks as possible – keeping yourself free to handle the next developments. Make it clear by your manner and tone that you are in charge. You welcome constructive, relevant suggestions but there is no time for argument or dithering.

7 Always keep the crisis in perspective. Keep your sense of humour and imagine yourself regaling your friends and colleagues with the drama. Taking this kind of approach helps you to stay calm and act logically. This may all seem like a nightmare now, but unless people are badly hurt, it's going to be a great story to dine out on when it's all over. Good luck!